Katabasis

Jay G Ying

smith|doorstop

Published 2020 by Smith|Doorstop Books
The Poetry Business
Campo House,
54 Campo Lane,
Sheffield S1 2EG
www.poetrybusiness.co.uk

ISBN 978-1-912196-30-2
Designed & Typeset by Utter
Printed by Biddles

Acknowledgements

Thanks to the editors of the following publications in which versions of these poems first appeared: *Modern Poetry in Translation*, *The Poetry Review*, *The North*, *Zarf*, *bath magg*, *The Scores*, *The Good Journal*, *The Adroit Journal*, *Fruit Journal*. I would like to acknowledge the various resources that have assisted my work: the Corpus of Sumerian Literature at the University of Oxford (JA Black et al, 1998-2006); the Sumerian Dictionary from the University of Pennsylvania (A Sjöberg, E Leichty, 2006); and *Inanna* by Diane Wolkstein and Samuel Noah Kramer (HarperCollins, 1983). I am grateful to Mary Jean Chan for judging the 2019 New Poets Prize, and to everyone who has helped with this pamphlet for their continued guidance and support.

Smith|Doorstop books are a member of Inpress: www.inpressbooks.co.uk. Distributed by NBN International, 1 Deltic Avenue, Rooksley, Milton Keynes, MK13 8LD.

The Poetry Business gratefully acknowledges the support of Arts Council England.

Contents

Two Conventions on Translation

Damaged, missing or untranslatable passages from one to several words in length are indicated by the mark ∗∗∗ (i.e. three asterisks).

Damaged, missing or untranslatable whole lines or passages are indicated as follows, on a new line:

(1 line damaged/missing/unclear)

(32 lines damaged etc.)

(unknown no. of lines damaged etc.)

*The 2001 military invasion and occupation of Afghanistan by the
United States, the United Kingdom, and its allies, known as Operation
Enduring Freedom (then Operation Freedom's Sentinel) was
originally named Operation Infinite Justice.*

*After all a photographer is a kind of spy bought by the highest
bidder, a parasite who lives off war without fighting it.*

– Mathias Énard

Forwarding

So Sister, what did you do in the War?

***

I burnt War's photographs over a grave by the fountain's dovecote.

In the hut on the mountains
the immaculate homing heralds were plucked bare;
   and War really was far flung. Dozen stamps

   of partitions or DMZs I could not believe still existed,
lapis lazuli ink from every ochre or synthetic resurrected in our
   tender address to endless War.

I moved a mountain over those testimonies of the dead, read each out
in a weak unsettling light.

So if War surely could travel back in time, back up the coast like
a forgotten word, stacking bodies in a mass grave of travertine

   well—War would only need to hear the wind's artefact
whistle, our oxidised soil upturned,
   War's lost heads cracking their jewels on hollowed-out houses
   searching for a neck to hang from inside.

It Was the Earliest Flight

It really was the earliest flight. The very first day after the very first night in the very first year of War. Eclipse light: barely any bodies emblazoned from that whitish flare of the lapis lazuli.

* * *

I stand up to loosen on the spot noticing War's hungry eyes sat near me stare back through all these sentinel stretches

And when I returned to that mortal realm, my muscles churning this way then that

I felt like a canary assessed as I relearn War's old death tango

From the great heaven she set her mind on the great below...

When you see the bomb's smoke, howl : When you go home, howl : When you enter his bedroom, howl : Father, do not let your daughter die in the War : Do not let your glossy daughter be fused with the hot metal of the War : Do not let your lapis lazuli become fantastically corrupted in the War : Do not let your limbs turn to precious metals in the War : Do not let your daughter be put to death in the War

Urgency

*When she entered the seventh gate : Her documents were
removed : What is this? : Silence! : The methods of War are perfect :
You cannot question them*

* * *

How can I get used to wearing this new face

I fumble out my ancient coins from all the slits they made upon my
body in Wartime just to feed them through the turnstile's tongue one
by one

In a stall I balance my flight ticket on the empty toilet roll dispenser
I sit down
I let myself have one trinket in my story at last

My organs were not done sheathing, and blood pulsed out of that
contemporary
wound where War had hung her hook into my numb flank, a lack I
only half recall

I forget to flush, to wash, to burn my bones, to scour out rust from
these strange
fingerprints

I meet my Sister's face in the mirror

(Was this really my new nose now?)

Hurrying as I hear the winds of men enter I wet my right hand to run
through my hair as knotted as black twitch grass

I see them see me do it in the reflection
my piercing shame bloomed like a blush, a character of lapis lazuli over
this fresh
lyric skin

When I close my eyes I am still so tired

I really felt like I was dreaming in that black cubicle again

With hope I read those cyphers cut into the wall as invitations towards
rituals

I was just as desperate, I had left my oak tree
I had the salt sea leave me
I loved
I wanted to love
I escaped the follies of love

I was my own curator of that erotic graffiti and behind each chipped
tile I saw War's
signage haunt me, one circuit eye drawn on watching me watch it
religiously

I think I shall either live or I shall die a ransom

I save a number on my phone

I save myself

I am surprised to find my bejewelled knife fished out from that white
cistern has survived sixteen hundred years without rust, restitution
or blunting

All that resentful time spent hiding from my Sister allowed that handle
to evolve
towards a more natural conclusion

This time, I will not kill War until I have heard the rest of their tale

From the great heaven the goddess set her mind on the great below ...

When she arrives at War's city she knocks on the door : She cries out in a voice that is as loud as the extraction of coal : Open up : Open up : I have been made to be alone : I demand my cut of War : When the Soldier of Fortune asks : Who are you? : She says : I am the Morning Star : On my way to the East : The Soldier asks : If you are the Morning Star on your way to the East : Why have you travelled to the zone : From which no civilian returns? : She replies : I have come to pay out our miners for their last breath : Avenge their blood in this ruined soil : And let their rites be sealed : The Soldier whispers : Stay here : I will speak to War : I will pass onto her your soft messages

My Name Is

Did it really happen? That descent into War? Sometimes they remember it as another sequence: a child falling down a mineshaft. Were they pushed by War, lured into it? In that airport that bears their name, all the glistening signs moan, surfaces of metal engorge underneath the bold death of the migrant worker's sun. That rich orb: it could be a familiar corpse the colour of lapis lazuli.

* * *

The plane lands late in the morning when I follow my procession into War's shining maw

A bird is never hollowed out, never accelerated, but cursed into its restless metal exile

Hearing the call distortion clean and concise on the tannoy

my name mispronounced, from that one command I can tell I was to march into her white gate

I was already late to that wherever-place I edged my stone eidolon towards
War

my flight ticket title misprinted, my mirror-life dependent on it

I was **INANNA, INANNA**, too hard to spell
twice yielded, reborn, doubled, made to be two bodies leaving or arriving, crossing by, lightly passing

Through every hair aroused then risen on the frontier of this new skin I found so unevenly before the dawn's interrogation

I tell myself off again for rarely sleeping, never two eyes closed

for not knowing any richer systems of poetry to halt those last nights,
each increasingly obscene catastrophe

From the great heaven Inanna set her mind on the great below ...

Naked and low : She entered War's throne room : War rose from her desk of maps : War's space was filled in almost immediately : Then from all sides the allies of War surrounded Inanna to pass their judgement : With their speech of loss : Fastened onto her naked body their eye of death : Their lines of wrath : They screamed at her : It was the sum cry of the guilty : Then War struck her : She was turned into a corpse : She was made to be inside out : A piece of rotting meat : A carcass to be hung from a hook on War's wall

Hostel

I fled to my skeleton bunk without warning

I sank into its foam and as I looked around I witnessed signs of the dorm's
other occupants littered on their sheets like loosened haloes

As if I were being crowded out by invisible ghosts
I heard the buzz of bass still playing from one headphone bud left above
and I found it unnerving to witness all those trinkets of sleep

> a map
> a silk scarf
> a ticket stub

> designer cases bursting like imported organs over
> the linoleum so near to me
> > layers of red fabric scattered like soft ore
> > travelling ceremonials out of reach on their beds

I had disturbed the room with my mortal presence
the navy sheet of the stained bedding over my knees like a borrowed skin

I knew I was soon to be walked upon,
> to be unmasked as an invader

Animal Vegetable Mineral

During parties in the War I remember my Sister would often point to my body dangling in her cave, inviting guests around to play a dangerous game of questions. Even when the party ended, when War turned off the lights, I could still hear their mocking laughter echo through the stones as I hung there in the darkness as still as a stolen oil painting.

*** *** ***

And on the flight it did not dislodge one bit, stuck inside my throat like a desperate seed

later when I unpack those wet articles of mine, as I unrolled clothes onto the hotel bed
not even remembering ever packing that shirt, these earrings, that knife

and I think back to a life when I believed: Is this all I had to show

the forever-presence of that legendary foreign wound in the background of my body like a catalogue from the stranger's flicking finger who itches to come out

In remission, I had pinned something alien down inside all along

I had held onto it like a painting from the walls of the clinic

I had smuggled that childish cabochon into Hong Kong

I let it build up during the course of my singular travels like an uncommon mould

And God I stared at what I had brought up in that toilet bowl almost halfway back to life

My black phlegm was as rotten as one long civilisation just ended,
marbled by that crude blood inside, veins not flecks, a leaf, never a jewel

From where in my organs did these metal islands burst

It would not wash down with the trickle of the automatic tap, refusing
to sense the jerk of my brown hand

(Was I a ghost?)

so with my nail I sickled that old mucus entity still plugging onto
eternity's rim

I imagined a wave to end it all

every corporeal cell swept away leaving only the imprint of life like a
daughter's blue hand on a cave door

I was disgusted by what had been quarantined within me

a little adjacent breeding so close to the speech I borrowed throughout
the day

Like a house, I hated myself for making it

pandemonium
that old Trojan Horse

My mistress abandoned heaven, abandoned earth,
and descended to the underworld ...

What has my daughter done : What have we done to the land : I have not
known a grief like this : Like ink from his finger : He fashioned the dirt into a
        (1 line unclear)
        : a creature neither male nor female : Like dirt from his finger : He
fashioned the ink into a
        (1 line unclear)
        : a creature neither female nor male : He gave them a sort of half-life
: He said : Go to War : Fly into the city : Enter through its doors like a pair
of drones

Welcome Home

When we lived with War we slept so close to that hot earth. There were many beds but zero doors. The polluted air from those vents burnt away all of our inside linings. I was only one contract away from becoming carbonised, one combustion away from melting down and turning into another conflict mineral.

*** *** ***

I encountered War in the trap streets they signed over.
Singed maps multiply out of my folded skin like a tablecloth
stained through with fresh white wine. I let War in; I let them
into my name just to tease me, to pretend War knows me.
Whenever a draught runs through the mosquito veils
it is as if a woman in white bolts towards the rockfall; a ghost
might miss those priceless bison etchings on the cave stone.
And past the blown off hinges on the door, past the men
grinding down their old molars in search of gold, as War
opens that damp wooden bunker ever so carefully, I wonder
if it had ever been locked in the first place. I had my doubts
when War cut out the lights, resulting in the extinction
of that pigmented mass herd. Thick beasts left their frame;
and there War stood, behind me, hot nostrils flaring down
my nape. I had my own theories about parietal art, omens
which I kept to myself like poison pills I forgot to bring
in times of War: the head of a rare white doe I would ration
for devouring later.

The Ninja

Escaping to our shared shower blocks
so early, too easily, I assumed no man
would catch me undress. I found his
towel on the rail, the door unlocked,
water sounds not falling quite far enough.

Sewn into the centre of the air, through
the tea stained curtain, I could make out
his appearing borders like a ghost in my
dream of lapis lazuli. Would he believe
I had been following him? Was he leading
me into another sweet trap? I could not

see clearly, not really; I left my glasses
on my bunk. I could only see a few steps
in front at a time, as if I were walking
through mist or steam, where every near
thing seemed one lost island away. As
unplaceable as an accent; as unmoored
as the strange passing seasons.

Inanna abandoned heaven, abandoned earth, and
descended to the underworld ...

    (1 line fragmentary)
War will offer you a gift : Refuse it : War will offer you an exit : Refuse it :
Ask War only for that body which hangs on that hook : If War says : That is
the body of the Morning Star : Say to War : Whether it is the body of our king
: Whether it is the body of our queen : Give us the body : And if War hands
over that cold body : Animate it with half of each life so the Morning Star can
rise : If only to find themself in War's precious and familiar grip once more

Miniatures

They flitted through the door like drones : They slipped through the door
like phantoms : The mother who gave birth : Was lying there : Uncovered
(3 lines missing)
Hair on her head collected like rotting flowers

* * *

I left all my slippery wet miniatures on the washing
machine lid, those lost travel sized bottles like toy
soldiers I would have to scoop up after the morning.
I clutched my dirty clothes to my chest like a bouquet
of limbs as I ran past that camera eye back towards
my dorm. During last night's dream I was a child again
by that classical hallway, journeying into the showers:
a newly sewn doll waiting to be filled up with sand.
On the ledge I witnessed three monstrous apples made
of metal, like heads in their dark display cases, turned
towards me. When I kissed one just to see if anything
might mutate, I found a century of grime greet me from
their temples. It was as if I had become the exiled body
soon to return; each tumorous dent or bruising gesture
revealed at the level of the lavish gems embedded in
every socket, each chanting trade secret planted along
waterways, troubled coasts bubbling like a rash of rust.

She abandoned her temples to descend to the underworld ...

(multiple lines missing)
So she was about to ascend from War : When the winds of War seized her : They said : Nobody leaves War unmarked : If you wish to return from War : You must provide a victor in your place : As she ascended from War : The winds clung to her : Hungry : Thirsty : Forgotten : Unmourned : Unloved : No children to kiss : Lovers shorn from lovers' arms : Children shorn from parents' knees : Bodies stolen from their homes : Still the winds clung to her : Not like warriors : But carrying maces nonetheless

Visible Waves

She is obsessed with the only photograph she smuggled out of her time in
War. Her skinned body hung from that kitchen hook like a wet pinkish
scarf, a dripping gift from a relative in the former colonies. War, in the
foreground, was still grieving for her husband back then; and her belly
was as gravid as a landmine, although you could not tell from how thin
War looked in that picture. No signs there were two people inside one.

* * *

A colony of water rails skulk past the same common
reeds of our house. I recall War's fingers taking it: one
empty egg War clutched whenever our coast shrugged
off its sawed yellow sedge; I could feel that water margin
grow cold on me like a second skin. Singed splinters out
of sight, ash on the lens of War's new black camera,
ornamental lintel stele floated face down, as the debris
hummed just above the river's surface like a drone of gnats.
Unseen, we pocketed the warped bullet shells smoking
in the rushes. But in my mind was there that drop of a
second body falling from the cliffs in the background
of that long exposure shot, the thud as someone hit
the sand, blood in the water? Long hair choked in mud
developed only in the blurry negative of a photograph.
I believed that distance must be the margin there: white
space which closes up, one character stamped down whose
name I did not know was so nearby, and another body –
was this one mine? A red beak where War's nose should be
as War's head turns slowly in the ink to face me now.

Cursed Resources

So War, what did you do to my Sister?

* * *

Post-War I always remembered the gold coin counterfeit
underneath my tongue would be the most useful metal.
It is a communal affair to bless the newly dead, transfuse
blood from a fake jewel in the maternity ward. On the path
out of the humanitarian hospital, fresh veins of blue seemed
to be the only medicine my ancestors sowed into miles of
stone. The cyanosed baby's lips are the colour of lapis lazuli.
The fibrotic lung of the miner underneath his autopsy lamp
is the colour of lapis lazuli. The puckered flesh of a stump
when exposed to air slowly rots, reconciles with the colour
of lapis lazuli. Never justice to be restored. Our crops near
the caves were bad, grainless, the weeping juice of leek stalks
as thin as widowed clacking asthmatics. Cricket wings jingle
from planted urns that when turned over turn around the heads
of murdered men. Last night, over our valley, a version of our
sky bloated before exploding: old fire crackers in peace time.
The drone of wind wailed through the insect nets scarcely
wide enough for only the women in our families. A cloche
of mist descended as if the rash on the lake divided, its gaps
breaking before reforming. Ghosts on fire swept past silvery
cedar figures like a glue you might find if you, in foreseeing
a surplus of blood, of credit at the turn of the century, slapped
each foreign metal mosquito with your palm; and saw she
had given birth to a stone child, eyes as quiet as lapis lazuli.

... *War, sweet is your praise.*

*She tore at her hair like esparto grass : She ripped it out like esparto grass :
Where is my child : Where is my man : Where is my Sister : Where am I
: Where*

(unknown no. of lines damaged)

✳ ✳ ✳

*I have been removed from the city : By the flies of the steppe : The wild bull
lives no more : I ask the hills and valleys : Where? : The jackal lies down in
the bed : The raven dwells in the flock of sheep : Ask me about the polluted
reeds : The wind must play it : Ask me for some sweet songs : The hot ghosts
must sing them : We are all captives in the steppe : Bound : The ewe gives up
her lamb : The goat gives up her kid : Every symbol translates in the morning*

✳ ✳ ✳

*She looked at the slain wild bull : She looked into his face : She said : The
face is yours : The spirit has fled*

✳ ✳ ✳

Grief in the inner chambers : As the characters wandered about the city like flies

✳ ✳ ✳

Who is your sister : I am your sister : Who is your mother : I am your mother

✳ ✳ ✳

*The fly circled her hair : And asked : If I tell you where War is : What will
you give to me?*

28